50 Last Supper Club Recipes

By: Kelly Johnson

Table of Contents

- Final Feast Beef Wellington
- Eternal Garden Ratatouille
- Last Bite Lobster Thermidor
- Ultimate Garlic Herb Roast Chicken
- Heaven's Honey-Glazed Ham
- Farewell Fettuccine Alfredo
- Final Hour Filet Mignon
- Divine Duck à l'Orange
- Endgame Eggplant Parmesan
- Last Call Crab Cakes
- Sunset Salmon en Papillote
- Closing Time Coq au Vin
- Parting Plate Pumpkin Risotto
- Last Dance Lamb Chops
- Twilight Tomato Basil Soup
- Goodbye Garlic Butter Shrimp
- Eternal Evening Egg Salad

- Final Hour French Onion Soup
- Last Supper Shepherd's Pie
- Farewell Flatbread Pizza
- Sunset Sweet Potato Gratin
- Closing Ceremony Caesar Salad
- End of Days Duck Breast
- Final Toast Tiramisu
- Parting Gift Pecan Pie
- Last Breath Beef Stroganoff
- Heaven's Harvest Vegetable Medley
- Final Flame Flat Iron Steak
- Sunset Scallop Skewers
- Last Sip Spiced Mulled Wine
- Goodbye Garden Gazpacho
- Final Flame Grilled Asparagus
- Parting Plate Pear and Blue Cheese Salad
- Last Hour Lobster Bisque
- Eternal Ember Eggplant Dip
- Closing Bell Chicken Marsala

- Farewell Fennel and Orange Salad
- Last Laugh Lemon Tart
- Final Cut Caprese Salad
- Endgame Enchiladas
- Last Slice Spinach and Feta Pie
- Twilight Trout Almondine
- Goodbye Garlic Mashed Potatoes
- Final Note Nectarine Cobbler
- Last Supper Sweet Corn Pudding
- Sunset Sesame Chicken
- Closing Curtain Chocolate Mousse
- Parting Plate Prosciutto Wrapped Melon
- Final Farewell French Macarons
- Last Word Wild Mushroom Risotto

Final Feast Beef Wellington
Ingredients:

- 2 lb beef tenderloin (center-cut)
- Salt and pepper to taste
- 2 tbsp olive oil
- 8 oz cremini mushrooms, finely chopped
- 2 cloves garlic, minced
- 2 tbsp fresh thyme leaves
- 4 oz prosciutto slices
- 1 sheet puff pastry, thawed
- 2 tbsp Dijon mustard
- 1 egg, beaten

Instructions:

1. Season beef with salt and pepper. Sear in hot olive oil until browned on all sides. Let cool.

2. Cook mushrooms, garlic, and thyme in a pan until moisture evaporates. Cool mixture.

3. Spread Dijon mustard over beef.

4. Lay prosciutto slices on plastic wrap; spread mushroom mixture over prosciutto. Place beef on top and roll tightly. Chill.

5. Roll out puff pastry, wrap around beef, seal edges. Brush with beaten egg.

6. Bake at 400°F (200°C) for 25-30 minutes until pastry is golden. Rest before slicing.

Eternal Garden Ratatouille

Ingredients:

- 1 eggplant, sliced into rounds
- 2 zucchinis, sliced into rounds
- 2 tomatoes, sliced into rounds
- 1 red bell pepper, sliced
- 1 yellow bell pepper, sliced
- 1 onion, thinly sliced
- 4 cloves garlic, minced
- 2 tbsp olive oil
- 1 tsp dried thyme
- 1 tsp dried oregano
- Salt and pepper to taste
- Fresh basil for garnish

Instructions:

1. Preheat oven to 375°F (190°C).
2. In a skillet, sauté onion and garlic in olive oil until softened. Spread evenly in a baking dish.
3. Arrange eggplant, zucchini, tomatoes, and peppers alternately over onion mixture.
4. Drizzle with olive oil, sprinkle thyme, oregano, salt, and pepper.

5. Cover with foil and bake 40 minutes. Remove foil and bake 10 more minutes.

6. Garnish with fresh basil before serving.

Last Bite Lobster Thermidor

Ingredients:

- 2 cooked lobster tails, meat removed and chopped
- 2 tbsp butter
- 1 small shallot, minced
- 1/4 cup dry white wine
- 1/2 cup heavy cream
- 1 tsp Dijon mustard
- 1/2 cup grated Gruyère cheese
- Salt and pepper to taste
- Chopped parsley for garnish

Instructions:

1. Preheat broiler.
2. Melt butter in pan, sauté shallots until translucent. Add wine and reduce by half.
3. Stir in cream and mustard; simmer until thickened.
4. Add lobster meat, salt, and pepper; cook 2 minutes.
5. Spoon mixture into lobster shells, top with Gruyère.
6. Broil until cheese is bubbly and golden. Garnish with parsley.

Ultimate Garlic Herb Roast Chicken

Ingredients:

- 1 whole chicken (about 4 lbs)
- 4 cloves garlic, minced
- 2 tbsp fresh rosemary, chopped
- 2 tbsp fresh thyme, chopped
- 1 lemon, halved
- 1/4 cup olive oil
- Salt and pepper to taste

Instructions:

1. Preheat oven to 425°F (220°C).
2. Mix garlic, rosemary, thyme, olive oil, salt, and pepper. Rub all over chicken and under skin.
3. Stuff lemon halves inside chicken cavity.
4. Roast chicken 1 hour to 1 hour 15 minutes, until internal temp reaches 165°F (75°C).
5. Rest before carving.

Heaven's Honey-Glazed Ham
Ingredients:

- 1 fully cooked ham (5-7 lbs)
- 1/2 cup honey
- 1/4 cup Dijon mustard
- 1/4 cup brown sugar
- 2 tbsp apple cider vinegar
- Whole cloves (optional)

Instructions:

1. Preheat oven to 325°F (165°C).
2. Score ham surface in diamond pattern and stud with cloves if desired.
3. Mix honey, mustard, brown sugar, and vinegar.
4. Place ham in roasting pan and brush glaze over ham.
5. Bake 1.5 to 2 hours, basting every 20 minutes until heated through and caramelized.

Farewell Fettuccine Alfredo

Ingredients:

- 12 oz fettuccine pasta
- 1/2 cup unsalted butter
- 1 cup heavy cream
- 1 1/2 cups freshly grated Parmesan cheese
- Salt and pepper to taste
- Fresh parsley for garnish

Instructions:

1. Cook pasta according to package, drain.
2. Melt butter in skillet, add cream and simmer 5 minutes.
3. Stir in Parmesan until melted and sauce thickens.
4. Toss pasta in sauce, season with salt and pepper.
5. Garnish with parsley.

Final Hour Filet Mignon

Ingredients:

- 4 filet mignon steaks (6 oz each)
- Salt and freshly ground black pepper
- 2 tbsp olive oil
- 3 tbsp butter
- 2 cloves garlic, smashed
- Fresh rosemary or thyme sprigs

Instructions:

1. Season steaks generously with salt and pepper.
2. Heat oil in skillet over high heat. Sear steaks 3-4 minutes per side.
3. Add butter, garlic, and herbs; baste steaks for 1-2 minutes.
4. Let rest 5 minutes before serving.

Divine Duck à l'Orange

Ingredients:

- 1 whole duck (about 5 lbs)
- Salt and pepper
- 1 cup fresh orange juice
- 1/4 cup sugar
- 1/4 cup white vinegar
- 1/2 cup chicken broth
- 2 tbsp Grand Marnier or orange liqueur (optional)
- 1 tbsp cornstarch mixed with 2 tbsp water

Instructions:

1. Preheat oven to 375°F (190°C).
2. Season duck with salt and pepper, roast about 1.5 hours until skin is crispy and internal temp is 165°F (75°C).
3. For sauce, caramelize sugar with vinegar until amber. Add orange juice and broth; simmer.
4. Stir in liqueur and cornstarch slurry until thickened.
5. Serve sliced duck with sauce.

Endgame Eggplant Parmesan

Ingredients:

- 2 large eggplants, sliced 1/2 inch thick
- Salt
- 3 cups marinara sauce
- 3 cups shredded mozzarella cheese
- 1 1/2 cups grated Parmesan cheese
- 2 cups all-purpose flour
- 4 eggs, beaten
- 3 cups breadcrumbs
- Olive oil for frying
- Fresh basil for garnish

Instructions:

1. Salt eggplant slices and let sit 30 minutes to draw out moisture. Rinse and pat dry.
2. Dredge eggplant in flour, dip in beaten eggs, then coat with breadcrumbs.
3. Heat olive oil in a skillet and fry eggplant slices until golden on both sides. Drain on paper towels.
4. Preheat oven to 375°F (190°C).
5. Spread a layer of marinara in baking dish. Layer fried eggplant, marinara, mozzarella, and Parmesan. Repeat layers ending with cheese on top.

6. Bake 35-40 minutes until bubbly and golden. Garnish with fresh basil.

Last Call Crab Cakes

Ingredients:

- 1 lb lump crab meat, picked over
- 1/2 cup breadcrumbs
- 1/4 cup mayonnaise
- 1 egg, beaten
- 1 tbsp Dijon mustard
- 1 tbsp Worcestershire sauce
- 2 green onions, chopped
- 1 tsp Old Bay seasoning
- Salt and pepper
- Olive oil for frying
- Lemon wedges to serve

Instructions:

1. In a bowl, gently mix crab meat, breadcrumbs, mayo, egg, mustard, Worcestershire, green onions, Old Bay, salt, and pepper.
2. Form mixture into 8 patties and chill 30 minutes.
3. Heat olive oil in skillet over medium heat; fry crab cakes 4-5 minutes per side until golden and cooked through.
4. Serve with lemon wedges.

Sunset Salmon en Papillote

Ingredients:

- 4 salmon fillets
- 1 lemon, thinly sliced
- 1 zucchini, julienned
- 1 carrot, julienned
- 4 sprigs fresh dill
- 2 tbsp olive oil
- Salt and pepper
- Parchment paper or foil

Instructions:

1. Preheat oven to 400°F (200°C).
2. Cut parchment into large squares. Place salmon in center.
3. Top each with lemon slices, zucchini, carrot, and dill. Drizzle with olive oil, season with salt and pepper.
4. Fold parchment to seal tightly creating packets.
5. Bake 12-15 minutes until salmon is cooked and vegetables tender.

Closing Time Coq au Vin

Ingredients:

- 1 whole chicken, cut into 8 pieces
- Salt and pepper
- 4 oz bacon, diced
- 1 onion, chopped
- 3 cloves garlic, minced
- 2 cups red wine
- 1 cup chicken broth
- 8 oz mushrooms, sliced
- 2 tbsp tomato paste
- 2 tbsp flour
- 2 tbsp butter
- Fresh thyme and parsley

Instructions:

1. Season chicken with salt and pepper. Brown bacon in a large pot, remove.
2. Brown chicken pieces in bacon fat, set aside.
3. Sauté onions, garlic, and mushrooms until soft. Stir in tomato paste and flour, cook 2 minutes.
4. Add wine and broth, scraping bottom. Return chicken and bacon, add thyme.

5. Simmer, covered, 45 minutes until chicken tender.

6. Stir in butter, garnish with parsley.

Parting Plate Pumpkin Risotto

Ingredients:

- 1 1/2 cups Arborio rice
- 4 cups chicken or vegetable broth, warm
- 1 cup pumpkin puree
- 1 small onion, finely chopped
- 2 cloves garlic, minced
- 1/2 cup dry white wine
- 1/2 cup grated Parmesan cheese
- 2 tbsp butter
- Olive oil
- Salt and pepper

Instructions:

1. Heat olive oil in pan; sauté onion and garlic until translucent.
2. Add rice, stir to coat. Pour in wine, stir until absorbed.
3. Add broth one ladle at a time, stirring constantly until absorbed before adding more.
4. When rice is creamy and almost tender, stir in pumpkin puree.
5. Add Parmesan and butter, season with salt and pepper.

Last Dance Lamb Chops

Ingredients:

- 8 lamb chops
- 3 cloves garlic, minced
- 2 tbsp fresh rosemary, chopped
- 2 tbsp olive oil
- Salt and pepper

Instructions:

1. Combine garlic, rosemary, olive oil, salt, and pepper. Marinate lamb chops 30 minutes.
2. Preheat grill or skillet over medium-high heat.
3. Cook chops 3-4 minutes per side for medium rare.
4. Rest 5 minutes before serving.

Twilight Tomato Basil Soup

Ingredients:

- 2 tbsp olive oil
- 1 onion, chopped
- 3 cloves garlic, minced
- 2 cans (28 oz each) crushed tomatoes
- 2 cups vegetable broth
- 1/2 cup fresh basil, chopped
- 1 tsp sugar
- Salt and pepper
- 1/2 cup heavy cream (optional)

Instructions:

1. Heat olive oil; sauté onion and garlic until soft.
2. Add crushed tomatoes, broth, basil, sugar, salt, and pepper. Simmer 30 minutes.
3. Blend soup until smooth.
4. Stir in cream if desired, heat through.

Goodbye Garlic Butter Shrimp

Ingredients:

- 1 lb large shrimp, peeled and deveined
- 4 tbsp butter
- 4 cloves garlic, minced
- 1 tbsp lemon juice
- Salt and pepper
- Fresh parsley for garnish

Instructions:

1. Melt butter in skillet over medium heat.
2. Add garlic and sauté until fragrant.
3. Add shrimp, cook 2-3 minutes per side until pink.
4. Stir in lemon juice, season with salt and pepper.
5. Garnish with parsley.

Eternal Evening Egg Salad
Ingredients:

- 8 hard-boiled eggs, chopped
- 1/4 cup mayonnaise
- 1 tbsp Dijon mustard
- 2 tbsp chopped fresh chives
- 1 tbsp lemon juice
- Salt and pepper to taste
- Optional: paprika for garnish

Instructions:

1. In a bowl, combine chopped eggs, mayonnaise, mustard, chives, and lemon juice.
2. Mix gently until combined.
3. Season with salt and pepper.
4. Chill before serving. Garnish with paprika if desired.

Final Hour French Onion Soup

Ingredients:

- 4 large onions, thinly sliced
- 4 tbsp butter
- 2 cloves garlic, minced
- 1 tbsp flour
- 6 cups beef broth
- 1/2 cup dry white wine
- Salt and pepper
- 1 baguette, sliced and toasted
- 2 cups grated Gruyère cheese

Instructions:

1. In a large pot, melt butter and sauté onions over low heat for 45 minutes until caramelized.
2. Add garlic and cook 1 minute.
3. Stir in flour, cook 2 minutes.
4. Add broth and wine, simmer 30 minutes. Season with salt and pepper.
5. Ladle soup into oven-safe bowls, top with toasted baguette slices and cheese.
6. Broil until cheese is bubbly and golden.

Last Supper Shepherd's Pie

Ingredients:

- 1 lb ground lamb or beef
- 1 onion, chopped
- 2 cloves garlic, minced
- 1 cup frozen peas and carrots
- 2 tbsp tomato paste
- 1 cup beef broth
- 3 cups mashed potatoes
- Salt and pepper
- 2 tbsp olive oil

Instructions:

1. Preheat oven to 400°F (200°C).
2. Heat olive oil, cook onion and garlic until soft. Add ground meat, brown.
3. Stir in tomato paste, broth, peas, and carrots; simmer until thickened. Season.
4. Transfer meat mixture to baking dish. Spread mashed potatoes on top.
5. Bake 20 minutes until golden.

Farewell Flatbread Pizza

Ingredients:

- 1 flatbread or naan
- 1/2 cup tomato sauce
- 1 cup shredded mozzarella
- 1/2 cup sliced mushrooms
- 1/2 cup sliced bell peppers
- 1/4 cup sliced black olives
- 1 tbsp olive oil
- Fresh basil leaves

Instructions:

1. Preheat oven to 425°F (220°C).
2. Spread tomato sauce on flatbread. Top with mozzarella, mushrooms, peppers, and olives.
3. Drizzle olive oil over top.
4. Bake 10-12 minutes until crust is crisp and cheese melted.
5. Garnish with basil leaves.

Sunset Sweet Potato Gratin

Ingredients:

- 3 large sweet potatoes, peeled and thinly sliced
- 1 cup heavy cream
- 1/2 cup grated Parmesan cheese
- 2 cloves garlic, minced
- 1 tsp fresh thyme
- Salt and pepper
- 2 tbsp butter

Instructions:

1. Preheat oven to 375°F (190°C).
2. Butter a baking dish, layer sweet potatoes evenly.
3. In a bowl, mix cream, garlic, thyme, salt, and pepper. Pour over potatoes.
4. Sprinkle Parmesan cheese on top.
5. Bake 45-50 minutes until tender and golden.

Closing Ceremony Caesar Salad

Ingredients:

- 1 large head romaine lettuce, chopped
- 1/2 cup Caesar dressing
- 1/2 cup grated Parmesan cheese
- 1 cup croutons
- Fresh cracked black pepper

Instructions:

1. Toss lettuce with Caesar dressing until evenly coated.
2. Add Parmesan and croutons, toss lightly.
3. Serve topped with cracked black pepper.

End of Days Duck Breast

Ingredients:

- 4 duck breasts
- Salt and pepper
- 1 tbsp five-spice powder
- 2 tbsp olive oil
- 1/2 cup red wine
- 1/4 cup orange juice
- 1 tbsp honey

Instructions:

1. Score duck skin, season with salt, pepper, and five-spice powder.
2. Heat olive oil in skillet, cook duck skin-side down 6-7 minutes until crispy. Flip and cook 3-4 minutes. Remove and rest.
3. Deglaze pan with red wine, orange juice, and honey; simmer until syrupy.
4. Serve duck sliced with sauce drizzled.

Final Toast Tiramisu

Ingredients:

- 6 egg yolks
- 3/4 cup sugar
- 1 cup mascarpone cheese
- 1 1/2 cups heavy cream
- 2 cups strong coffee, cooled
- 1/4 cup coffee liqueur (optional)
- 24 ladyfinger cookies
- Cocoa powder for dusting

Instructions:

1. Whisk egg yolks and sugar over a double boiler until thick and pale. Cool.
2. Fold mascarpone into yolk mixture.
3. Whip cream to stiff peaks, fold into mascarpone mixture.
4. Combine coffee and liqueur in shallow dish. Dip ladyfingers quickly, layer in dish.
5. Spread half mascarpone mixture over ladyfingers. Repeat layers.
6. Refrigerate at least 4 hours. Dust with cocoa powder before serving.

Parting Gift Pecan Pie

Ingredients:

- 1 unbaked 9-inch pie crust
- 1 cup light corn syrup
- 1 cup brown sugar
- 4 large eggs
- 2 tbsp melted butter
- 1 tsp vanilla extract
- 1/4 tsp salt
- 1 1/2 cups pecan halves

Instructions:

1. Preheat oven to 350°F (175°C).
2. In a large bowl, whisk corn syrup, brown sugar, eggs, melted butter, vanilla, and salt until smooth.
3. Stir in pecans.
4. Pour mixture into pie crust.
5. Bake 55-60 minutes until set and golden. Cool before serving.

Last Breath Beef Stroganoff

Ingredients:

- 1 lb beef sirloin, thinly sliced
- 2 tbsp butter
- 1 onion, chopped
- 8 oz mushrooms, sliced
- 2 cloves garlic, minced
- 1 cup beef broth
- 1 tbsp Worcestershire sauce
- 1 cup sour cream
- 2 tbsp flour
- Salt and pepper
- Cooked egg noodles

Instructions:

1. Melt butter in skillet, brown beef quickly, remove and set aside.
2. In same skillet, cook onion, mushrooms, and garlic until soft.
3. Stir in flour, cook 1 minute.
4. Add beef broth and Worcestershire sauce, simmer until thickened.
5. Return beef, stir in sour cream. Heat gently, do not boil.
6. Season, serve over noodles.

Heaven's Harvest Vegetable Medley

Ingredients:

- 1 cup broccoli florets
- 1 cup baby carrots
- 1 cup sliced zucchini
- 1 cup red bell pepper, sliced
- 2 tbsp olive oil
- 1 tsp garlic powder
- Salt and pepper
- Fresh parsley for garnish

Instructions:

1. Preheat oven to 425°F (220°C).
2. Toss vegetables with olive oil, garlic powder, salt, and pepper.
3. Spread on baking sheet and roast 20-25 minutes until tender and slightly browned.
4. Garnish with parsley.

Final Flame Flat Iron Steak

Ingredients:

- 1.5 lb flat iron steak
- 2 tbsp olive oil
- 3 cloves garlic, minced
- 1 tbsp fresh rosemary, chopped
- Salt and pepper

Instructions:

1. Rub steak with olive oil, garlic, rosemary, salt, and pepper.
2. Preheat grill or skillet to high heat.
3. Cook steak 4-5 minutes per side for medium rare.
4. Let rest 5 minutes before slicing.

Sunset Scallop Skewers

Ingredients:

- 1 lb large sea scallops
- 2 tbsp olive oil
- 2 cloves garlic, minced
- 1 tbsp lemon juice
- Salt and pepper
- Fresh parsley for garnish

Instructions:

1. Preheat grill to medium-high.
2. Toss scallops with olive oil, garlic, lemon juice, salt, and pepper.
3. Thread scallops onto skewers.
4. Grill 2-3 minutes per side until opaque.
5. Garnish with parsley.

Last Sip Spiced Mulled Wine
Ingredients:

- 1 bottle red wine
- 1 orange, sliced
- 4 cinnamon sticks
- 5 whole cloves
- 3 star anise
- 1/4 cup honey or sugar
- 1/4 cup brandy (optional)

Instructions:

1. In a large pot, combine wine, orange slices, cinnamon sticks, cloves, star anise, and honey.
2. Heat gently over low heat for 20-30 minutes, do not boil.
3. Stir in brandy if using.
4. Serve warm.

Goodbye Garden Gazpacho

Ingredients:

- 4 ripe tomatoes, chopped
- 1 cucumber, peeled and chopped
- 1 red bell pepper, chopped
- 1 small red onion, chopped
- 2 cloves garlic
- 3 tbsp olive oil
- 2 tbsp red wine vinegar
- Salt and pepper
- Fresh basil or parsley

Instructions:

1. Blend tomatoes, cucumber, bell pepper, onion, and garlic until smooth or slightly chunky.
2. Stir in olive oil, vinegar, salt, and pepper.
3. Chill at least 2 hours.
4. Garnish with herbs before serving.

Final Flame Grilled Asparagus

Ingredients:

- 1 lb asparagus, trimmed
- 2 tbsp olive oil
- Salt and pepper
- 1 lemon, zested and juiced

Instructions:

1. Toss asparagus with olive oil, salt, and pepper.
2. Grill over medium heat 5-7 minutes, turning until tender and charred.
3. Drizzle with lemon juice and sprinkle zest before serving.

Parting Plate Pear and Blue Cheese Salad

Ingredients:

- Mixed salad greens (5 cups)
- 2 ripe pears, thinly sliced
- 1/2 cup crumbled blue cheese
- 1/4 cup toasted walnuts
- 1/4 red onion, thinly sliced
- 3 tbsp olive oil
- 1 tbsp balsamic vinegar
- Salt and pepper to taste

Instructions:

1. In a large bowl, combine salad greens, pear slices, blue cheese, walnuts, and red onion.
2. Whisk together olive oil, balsamic vinegar, salt, and pepper.
3. Drizzle dressing over salad and toss gently before serving.

Last Hour Lobster Bisque

Ingredients:

- 1 lb cooked lobster meat, chopped
- 2 tbsp butter
- 1 small onion, diced
- 2 cloves garlic, minced
- 1/4 cup dry white wine
- 2 cups seafood stock
- 1 cup heavy cream
- 1 tbsp tomato paste
- Salt and pepper
- Fresh chives for garnish

Instructions:

1. Melt butter in a pot, sauté onion and garlic until translucent.
2. Add white wine and reduce by half.
3. Stir in seafood stock, tomato paste, and heavy cream. Simmer 15 minutes.
4. Add lobster meat, heat through without boiling.
5. Season with salt and pepper.
6. Garnish with chopped chives and serve hot.

Eternal Ember Eggplant Dip

Ingredients:

- 2 medium eggplants
- 2 cloves garlic
- 3 tbsp tahini
- 2 tbsp lemon juice
- 2 tbsp olive oil
- Salt and pepper
- Smoked paprika for garnish

Instructions:

1. Roast whole eggplants at 400°F (200°C) for 40 minutes until soft.
2. Let cool, scoop out flesh and discard skin.
3. Blend eggplant, garlic, tahini, lemon juice, and olive oil until smooth.
4. Season with salt and pepper.
5. Sprinkle smoked paprika on top and serve with pita or veggies.

Closing Bell Chicken Marsala

Ingredients:

- 4 boneless skinless chicken breasts, pounded thin
- Salt and pepper
- 1/2 cup all-purpose flour
- 3 tbsp olive oil
- 8 oz mushrooms, sliced
- 3/4 cup Marsala wine
- 1/2 cup chicken broth
- 2 tbsp butter
- Fresh parsley for garnish

Instructions:

1. Season chicken with salt and pepper, dredge in flour.
2. Heat oil in skillet, cook chicken until golden, remove and keep warm.
3. Sauté mushrooms in skillet until soft.
4. Add Marsala wine and chicken broth, simmer until reduced by half.
5. Stir in butter, return chicken to pan and coat in sauce.
6. Garnish with parsley and serve.

Farewell Fennel and Orange Salad
Ingredients:

- 1 bulb fennel, thinly sliced
- 2 oranges, peeled and sliced
- 1/4 cup pitted black olives
- 2 tbsp olive oil
- 1 tbsp white wine vinegar
- Salt and pepper
- Fresh mint leaves

Instructions:

1. Combine fennel, orange slices, and olives in a bowl.
2. Whisk olive oil, vinegar, salt, and pepper, then drizzle over salad.
3. Toss gently and garnish with mint leaves.

Last Laugh Lemon Tart

Ingredients:

- 1 prepared tart crust (9-inch)
- 1 cup sugar
- 3 eggs
- 1/2 cup fresh lemon juice
- 1/4 cup heavy cream
- Zest of 2 lemons
- Powdered sugar for dusting

Instructions:

1. Preheat oven to 350°F (175°C).
2. In a bowl, whisk sugar and eggs until smooth.
3. Stir in lemon juice, cream, and lemon zest.
4. Pour mixture into tart crust.
5. Bake 25-30 minutes until set.
6. Cool and dust with powdered sugar before serving.

Final Cut Caprese Salad
Ingredients:

- 3 large ripe tomatoes, sliced
- 8 oz fresh mozzarella, sliced
- Fresh basil leaves
- 3 tbsp extra virgin olive oil
- 1 tbsp balsamic glaze
- Salt and pepper

Instructions:

1. Arrange tomato and mozzarella slices on a plate, alternating.
2. Tuck basil leaves between slices.
3. Drizzle with olive oil and balsamic glaze.
4. Season with salt and pepper.

Endgame Enchiladas

Ingredients:

- 8 corn tortillas
- 2 cups shredded cooked chicken
- 1 cup shredded cheese (cheddar or Mexican blend)
- 1 cup enchilada sauce
- 1/2 cup diced onions
- 1/4 cup chopped cilantro
- Sour cream for serving

Instructions:

1. Preheat oven to 375°F (190°C).
2. Dip tortillas in enchilada sauce, fill with chicken, onions, and some cheese.
3. Roll up and place seam side down in a baking dish.
4. Pour remaining sauce over enchiladas and sprinkle with cheese.
5. Bake 20 minutes until bubbly and cheese melts.
6. Garnish with cilantro and serve with sour cream.

Last Slice Spinach and Feta Pie
Ingredients:

- 1 package phyllo dough (thawed)
- 2 tbsp olive oil or melted butter
- 1 lb fresh spinach, washed and chopped
- 1 cup crumbled feta cheese
- 1 small onion, finely chopped
- 2 cloves garlic, minced
- 3 eggs, beaten
- Salt and pepper to taste
- 1/4 cup fresh dill, chopped (optional)

Instructions:

1. Preheat oven to 350°F (175°C).
2. In a skillet, sauté onion and garlic in olive oil until soft. Add spinach and cook until wilted. Remove from heat.
3. Stir in feta cheese, eggs, dill (if using), salt, and pepper.
4. Lightly grease a pie dish. Layer about 6 sheets of phyllo dough, brushing each with olive oil or butter.
5. Pour spinach mixture over phyllo layers.
6. Cover with remaining phyllo sheets, again brushing each layer with oil or butter.
7. Bake for 30-40 minutes until golden brown and set.

8. Cool slightly before slicing and serving.

Twilight Trout Almondine

Ingredients:

- 4 trout fillets
- Salt and pepper
- 1/4 cup all-purpose flour
- 3 tbsp butter
- 1/4 cup sliced almonds
- 2 tbsp lemon juice
- 2 tbsp fresh parsley, chopped

Instructions:

1. Season trout fillets with salt and pepper, lightly coat with flour.

2. In a large skillet, melt 2 tbsp butter over medium heat. Cook trout skin-side down for 4-5 minutes until crispy, then flip and cook another 2-3 minutes. Remove and keep warm.

3. In the same skillet, add remaining butter and almonds. Cook until almonds are golden and fragrant.

4. Stir in lemon juice and parsley.

5. Spoon almond mixture over trout and serve immediately.

Goodbye Garlic Mashed Potatoes
Ingredients:

- 3 lbs russet potatoes, peeled and cubed
- 6 cloves garlic, peeled
- 1/2 cup heavy cream
- 4 tbsp butter
- Salt and pepper to taste
- Chopped chives (optional)

Instructions:

1. Place potatoes and garlic cloves in a large pot, cover with water, and bring to a boil. Cook until potatoes are tender, about 15-20 minutes.
2. Drain and return potatoes and garlic to pot.
3. Add butter and cream, mash until smooth and creamy.
4. Season with salt and pepper.
5. Garnish with chives if desired and serve warm.

Final Note Nectarine Cobbler
Ingredients:

- 5 ripe nectarines, sliced
- 1/2 cup sugar
- 1 tbsp lemon juice
- 1 tbsp cornstarch
- 1 cup all-purpose flour
- 1/2 cup sugar
- 1 1/2 tsp baking powder
- 1/2 tsp salt
- 6 tbsp unsalted butter, melted
- 1/2 cup milk

Instructions:

1. Preheat oven to 375°F (190°C).
2. In a bowl, toss nectarines with sugar, lemon juice, and cornstarch. Spread evenly in a baking dish.
3. In another bowl, combine flour, sugar, baking powder, and salt. Stir in melted butter and milk until just combined.
4. Spoon batter over the nectarines.
5. Bake for 35-40 minutes until topping is golden and cooked through.
6. Serve warm, optionally with vanilla ice cream.

Last Supper Sweet Corn Pudding

Ingredients:

- 4 cups fresh or frozen corn kernels
- 1 cup heavy cream
- 3 eggs
- 1/4 cup sugar
- 1/2 cup all-purpose flour
- 2 tbsp butter, melted
- 1 tsp baking powder
- 1/2 tsp salt

Instructions:

1. Preheat oven to 350°F (175°C).
2. In a blender or food processor, pulse corn and cream until slightly pureed but still chunky.
3. In a bowl, beat eggs and sugar. Stir in corn mixture.
4. Add flour, baking powder, salt, and melted butter; mix until combined.
5. Pour into a greased baking dish.
6. Bake 45-50 minutes until set and golden on top.
7. Let cool slightly before serving.

Sunset Sesame Chicken

Ingredients:

- 1 lb boneless, skinless chicken thighs, cut into bite-sized pieces
- 2 tbsp soy sauce
- 1 tbsp sesame oil
- 1 tbsp honey
- 2 cloves garlic, minced
- 1 tbsp ginger, minced
- 1/4 cup cornstarch
- 2 tbsp vegetable oil
- 2 tbsp sesame seeds
- 3 green onions, sliced
- Cooked rice, for serving

Instructions:

1. In a bowl, mix soy sauce, sesame oil, honey, garlic, and ginger. Marinate chicken pieces in this mixture for at least 30 minutes.

2. Toss marinated chicken in cornstarch until well coated.

3. Heat vegetable oil in a skillet over medium-high heat. Fry chicken until golden and cooked through, about 6-8 minutes.

4. Remove chicken and set aside. In the same skillet, pour remaining marinade, cook until slightly thickened.

5. Return chicken to skillet and toss to coat in sauce.

6. Sprinkle with sesame seeds and green onions.

7. Serve over rice.

Closing Curtain Chocolate Mousse

Ingredients:

- 6 oz bittersweet chocolate, chopped
- 3 large eggs, separated
- 1/4 cup sugar
- 1 cup heavy cream
- 1 tsp vanilla extract
- Pinch of salt

Instructions:

1. Melt chocolate in a heatproof bowl over simmering water, then let cool slightly.
2. Beat egg yolks with half the sugar until pale and thick. Slowly mix in melted chocolate and vanilla extract.
3. In another bowl, beat egg whites with a pinch of salt until soft peaks form, gradually add remaining sugar and beat until stiff peaks form.
4. In a separate bowl, whip cream until soft peaks form.
5. Gently fold egg whites into chocolate mixture, then fold in whipped cream.
6. Spoon mousse into serving dishes and refrigerate at least 2 hours before serving.

Parting Plate Prosciutto Wrapped Melon

Ingredients:

- 1 cantaloupe or honeydew melon, cut into wedges
- 8 oz thinly sliced prosciutto
- Fresh basil leaves (optional)
- Balsamic glaze for drizzling (optional)

Instructions:

1. Wrap each melon wedge with a slice of prosciutto.
2. Garnish with basil leaves if desired.
3. Drizzle lightly with balsamic glaze for extra flavor.
4. Serve chilled as an appetizer.

Final Farewell French Macarons

Ingredients:

- 1 cup powdered sugar
- 3/4 cup almond flour
- 2 large egg whites, room temperature
- 1/4 cup granulated sugar
- Food coloring (optional)
- Filling of choice (buttercream, ganache, or jam)

Instructions:

1. Sift powdered sugar and almond flour together.
2. Beat egg whites until foamy, gradually add granulated sugar and beat to stiff peaks. Add food coloring if using.
3. Fold dry ingredients into egg whites carefully until mixture flows like lava.
4. Pipe rounds onto parchment-lined baking sheets. Tap the tray to release air bubbles.
5. Let macarons rest at room temperature for 30-60 minutes until a skin forms.
6. Bake at 300°F (150°C) for 15-18 minutes. Cool completely.
7. Sandwich macarons with chosen filling. Chill before serving.

Last Word Wild Mushroom Risotto

Ingredients:

- 1 1/2 cups Arborio rice
- 4 cups vegetable or chicken broth, kept warm
- 1 lb wild mushrooms, cleaned and sliced
- 1 small onion, finely chopped
- 2 cloves garlic, minced
- 1/2 cup dry white wine
- 3 tbsp butter
- 1/2 cup grated Parmesan cheese
- 2 tbsp olive oil
- Salt and pepper to taste
- Fresh parsley for garnish

Instructions:

1. Heat olive oil in a large skillet. Sauté mushrooms until browned, remove and set aside.

2. In the same pan, melt 1 tbsp butter and cook onion and garlic until translucent.

3. Add Arborio rice and toast for 1-2 minutes, stirring constantly.

4. Pour in white wine and cook until mostly absorbed.

5. Add warm broth one ladle at a time, stirring frequently, waiting until liquid is mostly absorbed before adding more. Continue until rice is creamy and al dente,

about 18-20 minutes.

6. Stir mushrooms back in along with remaining butter and Parmesan cheese. Season with salt and pepper.

7. Garnish with parsley and serve immediately.

www.ingramcontent.com/pod-product-compliance
Lightning Source LLC
LaVergne TN
LVHW081319060526
838201LV00055B/2371